Caroline Arnold

ELECTRIC FISH

ILLUSTRATED BY
GEORGE GERSHINOWITZ

William Morrow and Company | New York 1980

Printed in the United States of America.
1 2 3 4 5 6 7 8 9 10

Library of Congress Cataloging in Publication Data

Arnold, Caroline.
  Electric fish.
  Summary: Discusses the fish that produce an electric current with a part of their body and others that are sensitive to electricity.
  1. Electric organs in fishes—Juvenile literature. 2. Fishes—Behavior —Juvenile literature. [1. Electric organs in fishes. 2. Fishes—Habits and behavior] I. Gershinowitz, George. II. Title.
QL639.1.A76   597'.019127   80-12479
ISBN 0-688-22237-4
ISBN 0-688-32237-9 (lib. bdg.)

The author wishes to express
her appreciation for his generous assistance
to Dr. Carl Hopkins,
Department of Ecology and Behavioral Biology,
University of Minnesota.

CONTENTS

1

What Is an Electric Fish?

Did you know that an electric eel can produce enough electricity to shock a horse? Did you know that a shark is able to find a fish hidden in the sand because it can feel a small amount of electricity given off by the fish? Did you know that some fish can "talk" to each other with electric signals? All of these fish have a unique sensitivity to electricity.

Some fish can produce an electric current. The electricity is made by a special part of the fish's body

5

called an "electric organ." The electric organ can be very big or very small. It works like the batteries in a flashlight. When it is turned on, there is a flow of electricity. You can press a button to make a flashlight go on and off. An electric fish can turn its batteries on and off too.

Some fish can "feel" electricity. They have special structures in their skin called "electric receptors." A receptor is something that receives something. An electric receptor receives electricity. All fish that have electric organs also have electric receptors. Some fish that have electric receptors, however, do not have electric organs.

Although you do not have electric receptors in your skin, you can sometimes feel electricity too. When you do, you say that you have gotten a shock. You can feel only relatively large amounts of electricity. Depending on the size of the current, the feeling varies from a slight tickle to a severe shock. Fish with electric receptors can feel much smaller amounts of electric current than you can.

Electric fish can be divided into three main types. First there are fish that can produce very large amounts of electricity, such as electric eels. Then there are fish that do not produce electricity but are able to feel it. Some of them are sharks and catfish. Last there are fish that produce very weak electric signals. They are the Nile fish, snout fish, and knife fish.

The Discovery of Electric Fish

Some kinds of electric fish have been known for thousands of years. Pictures of electric rays can be seen on ancient Greek pottery; the ancient Egyptians made hieroglyphs of electric catfish; and electric eels were known to pre-Columbian civilization in South America. All of these fish produce large amounts of electricity, which undoubtedly is why they received this attention. A shock from any one of them would have been memorable.

The ancient Greeks were the first people to study electricity. In one experiment they compared the shock produced by the electric ray with the static electricity produced when amber was rubbed with a piece of fur. The Greek word for amber is *electron,* from which the English word *electric* comes.

Not until the eighteenth century, however, did the modern study of electricity begin. In 1791, the Italian scientist Luigi Galvani did some experiments with the nerves and muscles of frogs and first demonstrated that animals could make their own electricity. The amounts of electricity produced by the nerves and muscles of animals is ordinarily very small while those produced by the electric ray are large. Still, Galvani suggested that they came about in the same way.

Then, around 1800, another Italian scientist named Alessandro Volta made a new contribution to the study of electricity. He invented the battery. Finally the mysterious force of the strongly electric fish began to be explained. People learned that fish like the eel, the ray, and the electric catfish had their own "batteries" that they could turn on and off at will. This discovery was amazing. No other kind of animal had been known to have this ability.

The electrical instruments of the eighteenth and nineteenth centuries were not nearly as sensitive as those of today. They were able to detect only fairly large amounts of electricity. The amount of electricity produced by weakly electric fish and received by fish with receptors was so small that it went unnoticed. Most of the research on weakly electric fish and on fish with electric receptors has been done since 1950.

Electricity: A Sixth Sense
When you think of your five senses you think of

8

sight, sound, touch, taste, and smell. You use your senses to learn about the world around you and to communicate with others. Electric fish have an additional sense, a sensitivity to electricity. They use their electric sense in many ways: for defense and capture of prey, for location of hidden objects, for navigation, and for communication.

Most fish that can produce electricity surround themselves with what is called an "electric field." Everything that is alive, including man, gives off small amounts of electricity in water, which is a good conductor. But a fish with an electric organ can produce a much stronger electric field than other living things. The signals that it sends go out in all directions. A diagram of an electric field looks like a series of circles. As the circles get bigger farther away from the source of the electricity (the fish), the electric force becomes weaker.

An electric fish that has both an electric organ and electric receptors can send signals to itself. When these electric signals pass through solid objects, they become changed. These changes give the fish information about that object. The fish can learn whether the object is big or little, near or far, alive or not, and many other things.

The diagram shows how an object can change

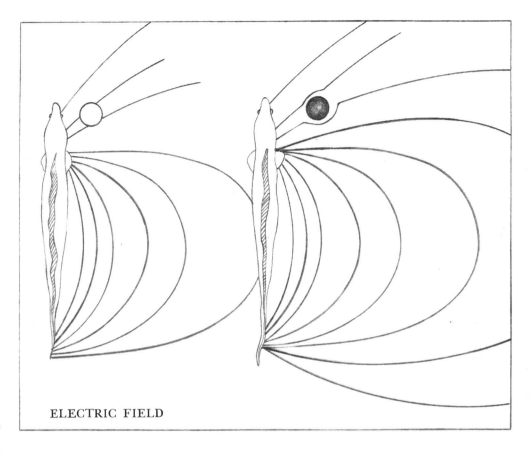

ELECTRIC FIELD

the shape of an electric field. Some objects conduct electricity better than others. The fish can feel this change in conductivity with its electric receptors. In this way an electric fish can "feel" objects nearby without actually seeing them. This ability is called "electrolocation."

Electricity in oceans and fresh water comes from several sources. One is from animals and fish in the water. Electric fields are also created by the movement of water over the Earth's magnetic field. Ocean currents, the tides, and even waves all produce electric fields in the ocean. Earthquakes and lightning can create electric fields in the water too.

Electric receptors can sense either changes in the electric field produced by a fish's own electric organ or it can sense electric fields produced by other things in the water.

Where Can You See Electric Fish?

The chances are that you will never see an electric fish in its natural environment. Most electric fish live in more tropical climates than ours. You may be able to see them, however, in an aquarium or in a park such as Sea World that features aquatic animals.

Sea World in San Diego, California, has displays of several kinds of electric fish, including an electric eel and some of the smaller knife fish and snout fish that are weakly electric. In each of the fish tanks two wires have been placed in the water. The wires are called "electrodes." They are connected to an amplifier and a loudspeaker so that if there is an electric discharge you will hear it as a series of clicks.

If you watch the weakly electric fish swim around in their tanks, you can hear their discharges. They sound a little like the static you sometimes hear on the telephone or radio. These fish discharge almost constantly, and you can listen to them at any time.

Each kind of electric fish has its own characteristic "sound." Some of the sounds have been compared to the trilling of a high flute. Others are more like an airplane engine. The sounds are different because each kind of fish has its own kind of electric signal.

The electric eel does not discharge its electricity very often. Most of the time it rests on the bottom of its tank, and the loudspeaker is silent. The eel has two kinds of discharges. When the eel is simply cruising around in its tank, you can hear a series of clicks similar to those of the weakly electric fish. These discharges come from a small electric organ at the tip of the eel's tail and are used for electrolocation. Only at feeding time does the eel turn on its large electric organ. The noise of this enormous discharge sounds like the exploding of a bomb compared to the other clicks.

Some aquariums that have displays of eels place a gauge that looks something like a large thermometer next to the eel's tank. The gauge measures the amount of electricity that the eel produces with each discharge. If you are lucky enough to see the eel discharging, you can watch the gauge to find out exactly how much electricity is being produced.

2

Strongly Electric Fish

The fish that can produce a lot of electricity are electric eels, electric catfish, electric rays, stargazers, and skates. All are strange-looking fish. The electric eel is a very long fish. Its tail is 90 percent of its length. Electric rays and skates look a bit like underwater bats. They glide gracefully over the bottom of the ocean with their winglike fins rippling in the water. Stargazers are unusual because their eyes are located on the top of the head

14

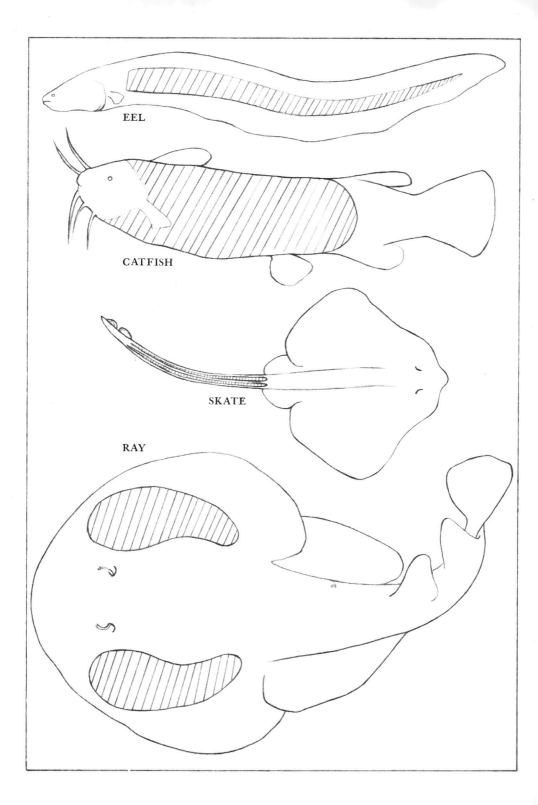

EEL

CATFISH

SKATE

RAY

and they seem to be permanently looking at the stars. The electric catfish is distinguished by a set of catlike whiskers. All of these fish use their electricity to obtain food or to defend themselves.

Electric Eels

The electric eel, which produces more electricity than any other living creature, is probably the best-known electric fish. It is found in the tropical streams and lakes of South America, and people who live there have held many superstitions about it. One of them was that if you touched an eel while chewing tobacco, you would not get shocked. Unfortunately, such protection does not work. They also believed that dried bits of eel could cure some illnesses.

The first European to study eels in their natural habitat was a man named Baron Alexander von Humboldt. Baron von Humboldt was a young German scientist eager to see the world. In 1799, at the age of thirty, he left Europe and sailed for South America. He spent five years there, exploring and studying, and he wrote a book describing his experiences.

As a scientist in Europe Baron von Humboldt had been interested in electricity. Therefore, he was particularly interested in seeing electric eels when he was in South America. However, the people who lived there were so afraid of being shocked by the eels that they refused to catch any for him, even though he offered a reward.

Finally Baron von Humboldt found a group of people to take him to a pool where eels were known to live. They then collected a group of about thirty horses and mules, which were forced into the pool. The eels became excited and re-peatedly shocked the horses and mules, severely disabling them. Finally the eels became tired and were easily caught.

At last Baron von Humboldt was able to see the electric eels about which he had been so curious. He wanted to feel the sensation of a shock from an eel, so he put his feet on top of one. Here is what he wrote about that experience: "I was affected during the rest of the day with a violent pain in the knees and in almost every joint." Clearly people had good reason to be afraid of electric eels.

Baron von Humboldt's studies of the eel have been important to modern medicine. They sug-gested that the eel was able to produce its electric shock because there was electricity going from its nerves to its muscles. Baron von Humboldt

17

overleaf: ELECTRIC EEL

thought that human muscles might also be activated by tiny amounts of electricity from the nerves. At that time there was no way for him to prove the theory, but we now know he was right.

The electric organs of the eel are inside the tail. There are three of them—one very large one and two smaller ones. The large organ produces the strong shocks that are used to kill prey or for defense. One smaller organ apparently acts as a trigger to set off the larger organ. The other small organ is at the tip of the tail and is used for electrolocation.

All the electric organs are made up of many tiny identical electric parts. Each part is called an "electroplate." There are five to six thousand electroplates in an electric eel. Each electroplate is like a very small battery. They are arranged one after the other like the batteries in a very long flashlight. You can imagine that if you had thousands of batteries connected together end to end that the result would be a lot of electricity. Even a small electric eel can produce a strong shock. Adult electric eels can produce up to 600 volts of electricity, more than enough to kill the frogs and small fish that are their food. An electric eel can also stun a man or even a horse easily.

Dr. Carl Hopkins, who studies weakly electric fish in South America, once accidentally caught several small eels in a fishnet. He said that touching the net was like putting his finger on an electric-light socket. In this case, even though the eels were out of water, the wet net conducted their electricity. These eels were only fifteen to twenty inches long while adult eels are often as long as six feet. Once an eel was caught that measured nine feet.

Dr. Carl Sachs, a scientist who studied eels, found that an electric eel could produce up to 150 shocks per hour, or two and a half shocks per minute, without becoming tired. Although each shock is strong, it lasts only two or three thousandths of a second.

Even though water is a good conductor of electricity, the strength of a shock becomes less farther away from the eel. The maximum effect is found close to the eel, within the distance that is equal to the length of the eel. Thus, a three-foot-long eel should be within three feet of its prey to give it the strongest shock. An eel is not dangerous to you unless you are close to it.

The large electric organ in the eel produces such an impressive amount of electricity that for many years the small electric organ at the tip of the tail was overlooked. This electric organ produces only about fifty volts. During the 1940's Dr. Christopher Coates at the New York Aquarium did some experiments with eels. He found that this small electric organ is turned on whenever the eel moves about. It helps the eel to "see" objects in its environment. This experiment was the first demonstration of a fish's electrolocation ability.

Although an eel is born with normal eyesight, it gradually loses its ability to see as it grows up. This loss does not seem to cause it any problems. It uses its small electric organ in its tail to locate objects and help find its direction. The electric eel's ability to guide its movements with electric signals instead of eyesight is so well developed that it can swim backward just as easily as it can swim forward.

An electric eel is also sensitive to electric signals produced by another eel. Electric eels will gather around the head of another that is discharging and look for food. In this way electric eels seem to use their electricity to communicate with each other. An eel that has just found food sends out shocks to stun the prey. Other eels seem to understand

22

that this behavior means that food is available.

The scientific name for the electric eel is *Electrophorus electricus*. All living things have scientific names. The first part of the name indicates the genus of the animal or plant. The second part indicates the species. Thus, the electric eel belongs to the genus *Electrophorus* and the species *electricus*. Living things that are closely related in their genus and species are grouped into families. Families that are closely related are grouped into orders, and closely related orders are grouped into classes.

The electric eel is in the family of gymnotid fish. Probably the electric organ of the eel was once very small like those of the other gymnotid fish. Over millions of years, however, it evolved gradually into a more and more powerful organ until it became the super electric organ it is today.

Electric Catfish

Next to the electric eel, the electric catfish is the most powerful producer of electricity. It lives in the rivers and lakes of tropical Africa and in the Nile River valley. The scientific name of the electric catfish is *Malapterurus electricus*. Although

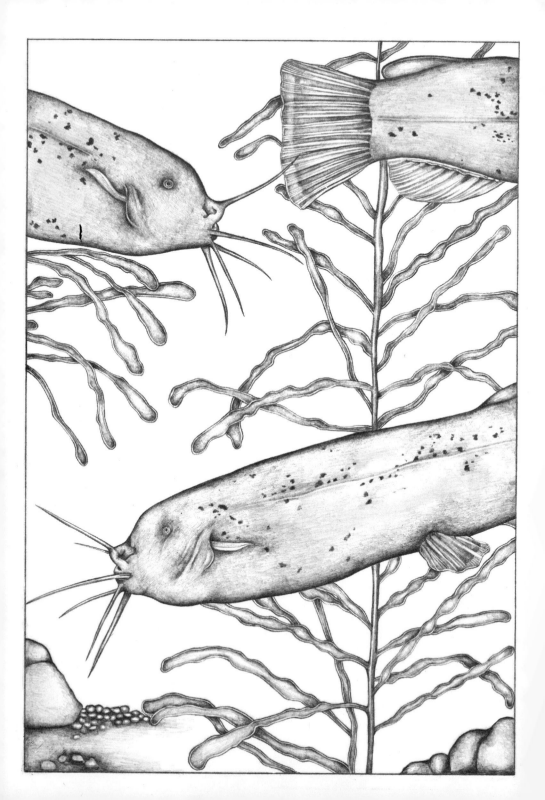

there are many kinds of catfish all over the world, this one is the only kind that is able to produce electricity.

Electric catfish may grow to be nearly four feet long. A small fish from four to eight inches long can produce only about 80 volts of electricity, but a large fish can produce an amount up to 350 volts.

Like the electric eel, the electric catfish uses its ability to shock to obtain food and to defend itself. Electric catfish are not fussy eaters. They will eat almost any kind of animal food they can find along the river and lake bottoms where they live.

The electric organ of the catfish is formed from a layer of muscle just under the skin of its body. It is divided up into many compartments with electroplates inside each one. Each electroplate produces a tiny amount of electricity. When the electric organ is turned on, all the tiny amounts of electricity are added together to produce one big shock.

Depictions of electric catfish appear in ancient Egyptian paintings and tomb carvings as early as 2750 B.C. The hieroglyph that represented the catfish meant "He who releases many." Any fisherman who accidentally caught a catfish in his net

25

and touched it would be so shocked he would drop the whole net full of fish back into the water, thus "releasing many."

Electric catfish have been used for hundreds of years in Africa as a cure for headaches and other ailments. The sick person would touch the catfish and get a shock. Sometimes the headache would go away. The people who used this treatment did not know that similar shock therapy would become a major feature of modern medicine.

Electric Rays

After electric eels and electric catfish, electric rays are the most powerful producers of electricity. They are found throughout the ocean except where the water is very cold. A large ray can produce two hundred volts of electricity. Small rays produce fifty to sixty volts. Fifty volts are enough to electrocute a large fish.

The salt water of the ocean is a better conductor of electricity than fresh water. Thus, electric fish that live in the ocean, such as the rays, do not need to produce as much electricity to create an effective shock as electric fish that live in fresh water.

There are three dozen different species of

electric rays. All of them have the scientific family name of Torpedo. The largest electric ray can grow to be five feet long and two hundred pounds. The smallest is only seventeen inches long. The famous sting ray does not belong to the Torpedo family and is not electric.

Rays are distant relatives of the shark. Their bones, like those of sharks and skates, are made of cartilage, and their scales are very small. All fish with such bones belong to a class called Chondrichthyes, or Elasmobranchs. Fish with calcified bones and scales belong to the class called Osteichthyes.

The shape of the ray is much different from that of its relative the shark. The ray's body has become greatly flattened, and its sides reach out like giant wings. A gentle rippling of these "wings" propels the ray through the water. It glides along so smoothly it seems to be an eerie underwater spaceship.

Like electric eels and electric catfish, electric rays use their electricity to obtain food, but their method is different. An electric ray pounces on its victim, wraps it with its winglike fins, and then shocks it. Rays typically eat fish and small sea animals such as crabs and shrimp.

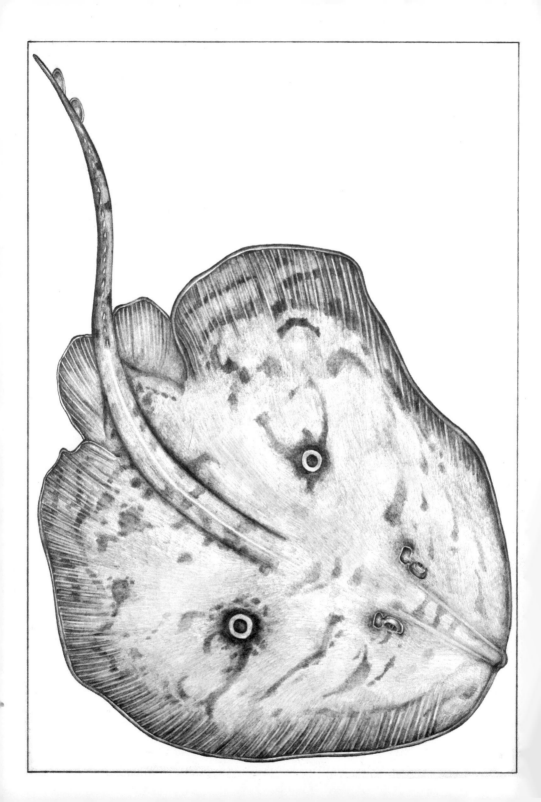

The electric system of the ray is arranged somewhat differently from that of the eel or catfish. The ray has two large electric organs on either side of its head. These organs are made up of many small columns. Each column is made of tiny electroplates and acts like a battery. In a large ray there may be as many as half a million electroplates in each column. The columns are arranged side by side rather than end to end as in the eel.

Like the eel, a ray also has a small electric organ in its tail. It is not used to capture prey. No one knows exactly how it is used. Perhaps, like the electric eel, the ray uses it for electrolocation.

Rays have been around for millions of years. A rare fossil of a sting ray, a relative of the electric ray, has been found that is fifty-eight million years old. There are pictures of electric rays painted on ancient Greek pottery. Although the ancient Greeks and Romans did not understand how the ray produced its electric shock, they recognized that it had peculiar properties.

The Romans used electric rays to treat gout, headaches, and other diseases. They either had the patient stand on the live electric ray, or else they wrapped the ray around the patient's head. Can

you imagine having an electric ray wrapped
around your head to cure a headache?

Stargazers

Stargazers produce about fifty volts of electricity.
There are over twenty species of them, some as
long as sixteen inches. They all belong to the
family with the scientific name Uranoscopid. This
Latin word means "to look at the heavens." Stargazers are found mainly along the western coast of
the North and South Atlantic.

A small electric organ is found behind each eye
of a stargazer. Scientists do not know what the main
purpose of this electric organ is. It may be used
for communication during the mating season. It
may help to subdue captured prey. They do know
that it turns on when the fish is eating. It also
seems to help defend the fish against enemies.
Anything touching a stargazer when its electric
organs are turned on will certainly be shocked
enough to let go and leave it alone.

Stargazers apparently do not use their electric
organ to obtain food. They have another method.
A stargazer buries itself in the sand or mud at the
bottom of the ocean. It leaves only its eyes and
nostrils showing, which is why its eyes are on top

30

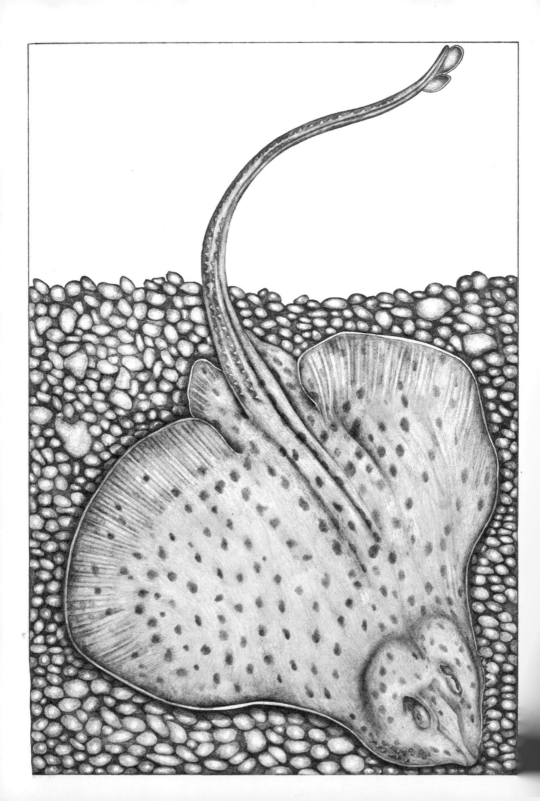

of its head. If they were on the side like those of most fish, it could not see. As soon as a likely piece of food comes by, such as a crab or a small fish, the stargazer opens its mouth and snaps it up.

Skates

There are many kinds of skates. Like the rays, they are relatives of sharks. They belong to the family with the scientific name Rajid. Skates can be found in most parts of the ocean except where it is very cold.

Skates are flat like electric rays. Unlike an electric ray, however, a skate does not have an electric organ in the main part of its body. Its only electric organ is in its tail. The amount of electricity produced by this electric organ varies from one kind of skate to another, but the most that has ever been recorded is about four volts.

No one knows what purpose the skate's electric organ serves. Possibly it is used for electrolocation. Possibly it is used for communication. Scientists will have to study the skate more to find out exactly what its function is.

33

3

Fish That Can "Feel" Electricity

The fish that are able to "feel" electricity in the
water include sharks and rays, catfish, paddlefish,
and possibly salmon and eels. Most of these fish
have those structures in their skin that are called
"electric receptors." Using them to sense electricity, the fish can find food, detect objects,
and navigate over long distances. There are
several kinds of electric receptors in fish, but
all of them can detect tiny amounts of electricity.

34

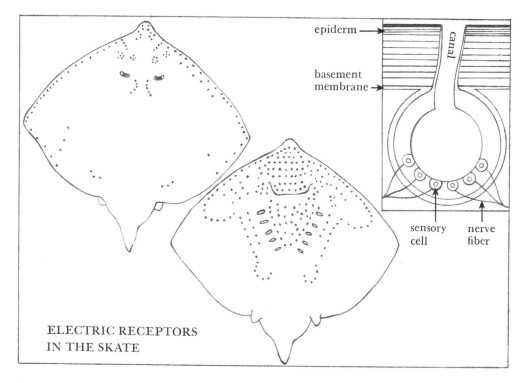

epiderm

basement
membrane →

canal

sensory
cell

nerve
fiber

ELECTRIC RECEPTORS
IN THE SKATE

The ampullae of Lorenzini are shown by black dots. On the left above is a top view of the skate, and under it is a view of the skate from below. Inset: cross-sectional drawing of a typical ampullary receptor.

Sharks, Rays, and Skates

Sharks, rays, and skates are all in the class of Elasmobranch fish. All the Elasmobranch fish have electric receptors in their skin. These receptors are called "ampullae of Lorenzini." The ampullae of Lorenzini are tiny tubes filled with a jellylike substance. One end of the tube is on the surface of the fish's skin, and the other is inside its body. Small amounts of electricity in the water are

35

transferred through the tubes to the inside of the fish's body.

As early as 1935 sharks had been thought to be sensitive to electricity, but not until 1971 was it finally proved. A Dutch scientist named Dr. A. J. Kalmijn did an experiment that clearly showed that sharks and rays can find a fish using only their electric sense. Here is what he did.

Dr. Kalmijn kept the sharks and rays in small swimming pools. He fed them with small flatfish, because he knew that flatfish were part of their usual diet. The flatfish would typically bury themselves in the sand at the bottom of the pool. When a shark or ray was hungry, it would swim around the pool. Suddenly it would uncover the flatfish, grab it, and take it away and eat it.

Dr. Kalmijn wanted to find out how the shark knew where to find the buried flatfish. The shark could not have seen it because it was totally covered with sand. However, Dr. Kalmijn wanted to be sure that the shark did not use other clues, such as the smell of the flatfish or its movement under the sand, to find it. So he devised a special container out of gelatin for the flatfish. It was like a box made from unflavored jello. The gelatin chamber prevented the shark from seeing, smell-

36

FISH USED IN DR. KALMIJN'S EXPERIMENTS

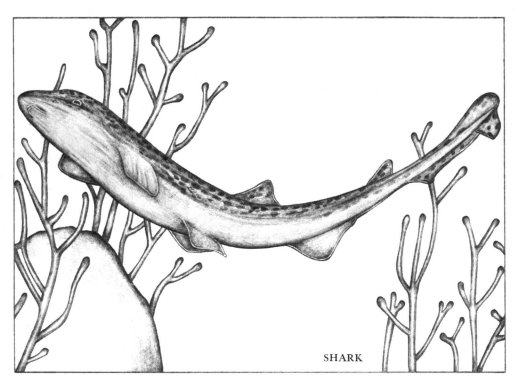

SHARK

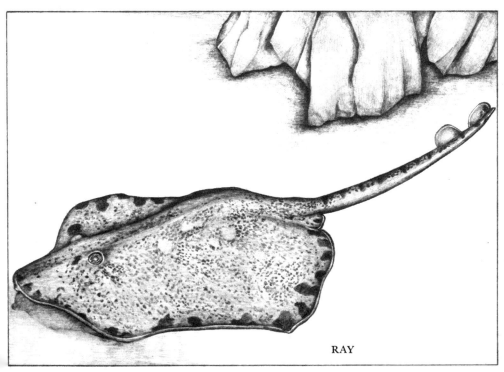

RAY

ing, or feeling the flatfish, but it did let through electricity. Like all living things in water, the flatfish produces a very weak electric field around itself.

When the flatfish in the gelatin chamber was put into a pool with a hungry shark or ray, the shark or ray tried to uncover it and eat it. The only way the shark or ray could have discovered the location of the fish was by "feeling" its electric field.

As a final proof of his experiment, Dr. Kalmijn buried two electric wires that created an electric field similar to that of the flatfish in the sand. The hungry shark or ray tried to uncover the fake fish (the electric wires) in the same way it had gone after a real fish.

The two species on which Dr. Kalmijn did his experiments were a small shark, *Scyliorhinus canicula*, and a ray, *Raja clavata*. He also felt that similar results would be obtained with other Elasmobranch fish.

Possibly sharks, rays, and skates use their electric sense to find their way about the ocean. Scientists know that the ampullae of Lorenzini are sensitive enough to detect electric fields created by ocean currents. Now they will have to study the Elasmobranch fish more to find out whether or not they

38

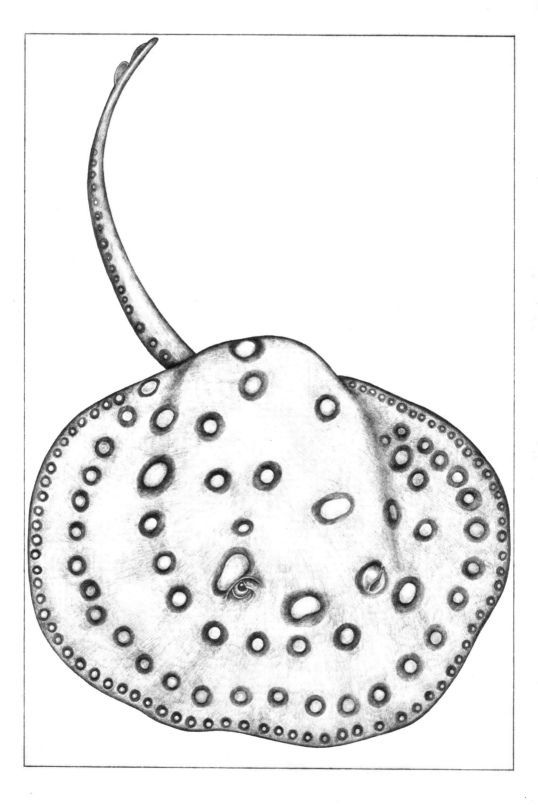

use their electrical sensitivity for navigation.

There is one ray that does not live in the ocean as other rays do. It is found in the rivers and streams of South America. This ray's scientific name is *Potamotrygon circularis*, but it is commonly known as the Amazon ray. Its electric receptors are tiny, almost invisible pores in its skin. Like its relatives that live in the ocean, the Amazon ray uses its electric sense to find food.

Catfish

Catfish are another group of fish that are sensitive to electricity. They belong to the order called Siluriformes. Many species of catfish are found all over the world.

Catfish have been observed to behave very strangely just before an earthquake. In 1932, two Japanese scientists, Dr. Hatai and Dr. Abe, suggested that catfish might be able to predict earthquakes. Scientists do not know for sure if this theory is possible, although there have been many reported instances of animals behaving oddly just before an earthquake occurs.

Scientists have tried to discover how catfish use their electric sense for their own needs. Probably catfish use their sensitivity to electricity in the

40

water to find their way around in the lakes and rivers where they live. Electric fields in the water can change near the shore, behind a barrier, where the water is deep, or where it is moving. If a catfish is used to orienting itself to electric fields, it might become confused and nervous when those fields change as they do just before an earthquake.

Dr. Kalmijn, who did the experiments on sharks and rays, also studied the catfish. He found that a catfish was able to use its electric sense to find a goldfish in the same way that sharks and rays use their electric sense to find food.

With one exception, all catfish have tiny ampullary receptors in their skin. *Plotosus,* the only saltwater catfish, has receptors with long tubes, similar to those of sharks and rays. In general, electroreceptive fish that live in salt water have ampullary receptors with long tubes, while electroreceptive fish that live in fresh water have ampullary receptors with very short or nonexistent tubes.

Paddlefish
The paddlefish, or spoonbill, which lives in the Mississippi River, is another fish that is sensitive to electricity. The scientific name for the paddle-

42

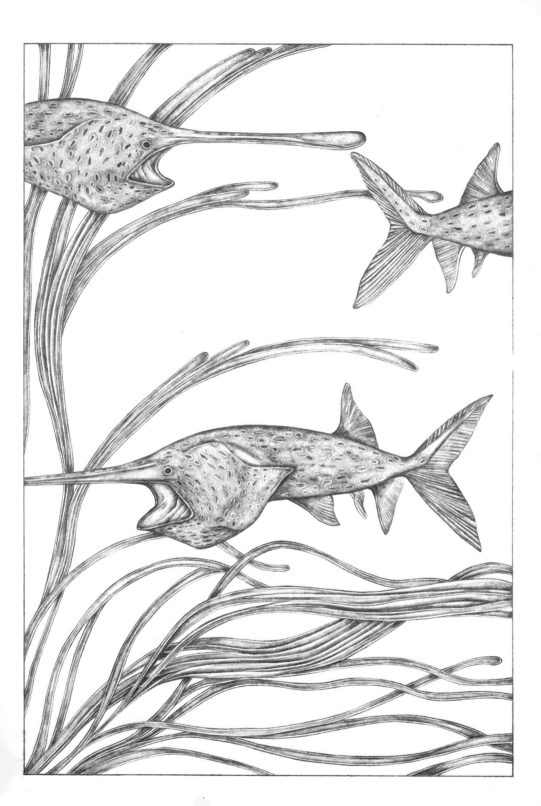

fish is *Polydon spathula*. It has on its head very tiny electric receptors that are called "primitive pores." Scientists do not know what purpose the paddlefish's electric sense serves. It may be to locate food, or it may be to locate other paddlefish. Paddlefish go around in groups, or schools. They cannot see very well, yet they never bump into each other. Perhaps they "see" each other with their electric sense.

There may be other kinds of fish with an electric sense that have not yet been discovered. Many fish, such as salmon and common eels, migrate over long distances each year. Possibly they use electric fields in the ocean to guide them to their destinations. Common eels are known to be sensitive to very small amounts of electricity, even though they have no obvious electric receptors. Future scientific research will reveal if there are other kinds of fish that are sensitive to electricity as well.

4

Weakly Electric Fish

There are over two hundred species of weakly electric fish. Most of them do not have common names, although their family groups are known by the common names of the Nile fish, snout fish, and knife fish. The Nile fish and snout fish live in Africa, and the knife fish live in South America.

Some of the snout fish and knife fish appear to be remarkably similar, even though they are not related to each other. When two unrelated animals

45

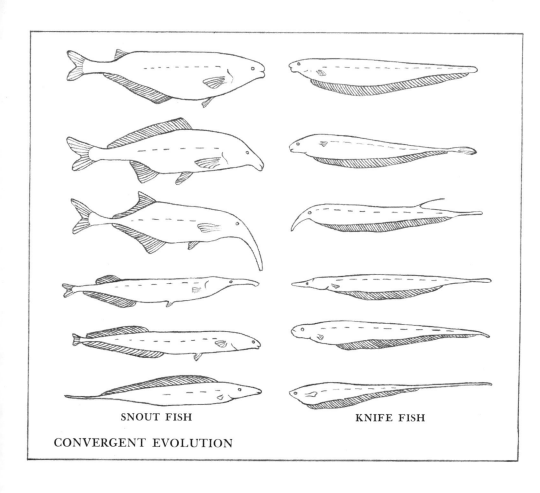

SNOUT FISH   KNIFE FISH

CONVERGENT EVOLUTION

develop the same kind of habits and appearance
in order to adapt to similar environments, scientists
call this phenomenon "convergent evolution."

Some species of knife fish were identified as
early as 1644. Drawings of some of the snout fish
can be found in ancient Egyptian tombs. But only
in this century have the details of the lives of
weakly electric fish been revealed.

46

Weakly electric fish use their electric sense for electrolocation and for communication. They have both electric organs and electric receptors. Their electric organs are tiny and can produce only three tenths of a volt of electricity or less.

Their electric receptors are of two types. One is an ampullary receptor similar to those found in other freshwater electroreceptive fish. The other is called a "tuberous" receptor and is located just under the surface of the skin.

Most strongly electric fish also use their electric sense to locate objects. But the function of electricity for communication in weakly electric fish was an exciting new discovery. Never before had anyone known of animals that could "talk" to each other with electricity. Scientists who study communication in electric fish hope that their findings will help us to learn more about how our own brains work.

To try to understand how fish could communicate with each other electrically, you can imagine the electric signal as a buzz. By varying the sound and the pitch of this buzz, a fish can send a coded message. The buzz can also be quickly switched off and on.

Fish do not hear or see the electric impulses.

They "feel" them electrically. Human beings do not have this electric sense. Therefore, electronic devices are used to convert the electric impulses into something that can be seen or heard.

A picture of the signals sent out by electric fish can be made by playing recordings of the signals into a machine called an "oscilloscope." The electric signals can also be converted to sound by amplifying them and playing them through a loudspeaker. The sounds for each species are quite different.

There are two basic types of sounds or pictures produced by the signals of weakly electric fish. Some species send out a signal that looks like a continuous band. They are called "tone" or "wave" fish. Some species produce a signal that looks like a series of separate blips. They are called "pulse" fish. All the snout fish are pulse fish. The Nile fish is the only African electric fish with a wave signal. The knife fish have signals of both types.

The Nile Fish

The Nile fish is found in the Nile River and in the lakes and streams of West Africa. It was the first weakly electric fish to be definitely identified.

The scientific name for the Nile fish is

Gymnarchus niloticus. Gymnarchus means "naked tail" in Latin, and *niloticus* means "from the Nile." You can see that this fish, unlike most other kinds, has no large fin on its tail. Its tail is different from that of an ordinary fish in another way too. Inside it is a small electric organ. This organ was first discovered in 1847 by Michael Pius Erdl, a German scientist at the University of Munich. He could not imagine how such a tiny electric organ could be used. It was obviously too small to produce a shock. For over a hundred years it was called "pseudoelectric," because everyone thought that it did not act like an electric organ, although it looked like one. The word *pseudo* means "fake."

Then, in the 1950's, an English scientist named Dr. Hans W. Lissman studied the Nile fish again. In 1951, he had brought a Nile fish from Africa to his laboratory in Cambridge, England. There he watched the fish swim around in its tank. As a Nile fish swims it keeps its body rigid and the long fin along its back ripples gracefully from side to side. As Dr. Lissman watched the Nile fish he noticed that it maneuvered gracefully among the objects placed in the tank. He also noticed that it easily caught the small fish that were put into the tank for food and could swim backward just as easily as it could swim forward.

Dr. Lissman was interested in finding out how the Nile fish could swim so well, since he knew that it has rather poor eyesight. The idea occurred to him that the pseudoelectric organ in the tail might not be "fake" at all. It could possibly be a detecting device. To test his theory, Dr. Lissman put into the water a pair of electrodes (two electric wires) that were connected to an amplifier. He knew that if there was any electricity in the water, the electrodes would pick it up. The electrodes did show that the fish was producing electricity and, in fact, that it was producing it all the time. This finding was not exactly what Dr. Lissman had expected. He thought that he might find short, sudden bursts of electricity similar to those of the eel. Instead, the Nile fish seemed to keep its electric organ turned on all the time.

Dr. Lissman decided to test several other fish with pseudoelectric organs. He found that members of the snout fish group and the knife fish group also emitted tiny amounts of electricity. They too kept their electric organs turned on all the time. Dr. Lissman's discoveries were the beginning of research on weakly electric fish.

50

With another scientist, Dr. Kenneth Machin, Dr. Lissman did some experiments to prove that the Nile fish used its electric sense to locate objects. In the first experiment they put two ceramic pots into the fish tank. One pot was filled with a substance that would conduct electricity, and the other pot was filled with a substance that would not. Behind the pot that conducted electricity they put a small piece of food. The Nile fish soon became trained to always look for food behind it. In later experiments Dr. Lissman and Dr. Machin learned that the Nile fish could tell the difference between a substance that conducted more electricity and one that conducted less, even if the difference was very small. Because the two pots always looked the same, the only way the Nile fish could tell the difference between them was by feeling the difference electrically.

When Dr. Lissman compared the brain of the Nile fish with the brain of a typical nonelectric fish, he found that parts of it were much bigger. These parts were the areas that are associated with the electric sense.

Snout Fish

The Nile fish and the snout fish are closely re-

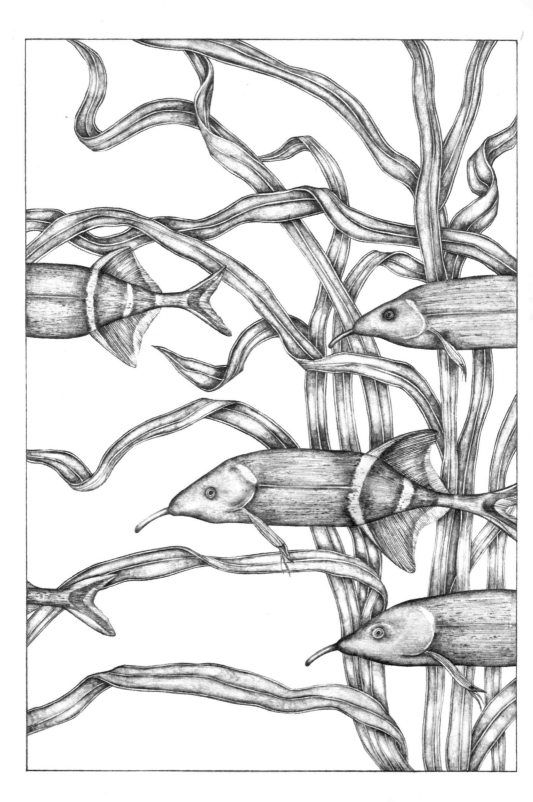

lated and belong to the order called Mormyriformes. Snout fish are in the family of mormyrid fish, which includes nearly two hundred species. Sometimes known as elephant-nose fish or baby whales, snout fish often have long snouts that they use to root around for food in the bottoms of the streams and ponds where they live.

Dr. Lissman did an interesting experiment with two snout fish of the same species. It suggested for the first time that electric fish communicate with each other. He placed a cloth divider in a fish tank so the fish could not see each other but could feel each other's electric impulses. When one fish increased the rate of its electric signals after being touched with a glass rod, the other fish responded by increasing its own rate. When the first fish was removed from the tank, the other fish did not respond when the glass rod was put into the empty side of the tank. This result indicated that the fish was responding to the other fish and not to the glass rod.

Knife Fish

One of the most interesting early discoveries about weakly electric fish was that all members of the same species use the same electric signal. In other words, each species of electric fish seems to have its own "channel." Thus, one fish can tell if another fish is of the same species as itself if their electric signals are the same.

Although all fish of a certain species operate on the same channel, there may be small differences among individuals. In 1963, two Japanese scientists, Dr. Watanabe and Dr. Takeda, studied a knife fish called *Eigenmannia virescens*. This fish belongs to the gymnotid family, the same family to which the electric eel belongs. Gymnotid fish live in Central and South America and are commonly known as knife fish because of the slender knifelike shape of their body. Most knife fish do not have common names.

Dr. Watanabe and Dr. Takeda found that when one Eigenmannia meets another with a signal very close to its own channel, each fish changes its channel slightly so that it no longer overlaps with that of the other fish. This ability has since been given the name "jamming-avoidance response." When two radio signals get confused, they are said to be jammed. The jamming-avoidance response reduces confusion between two fish with similar signals.

The discovery of this response suggested how

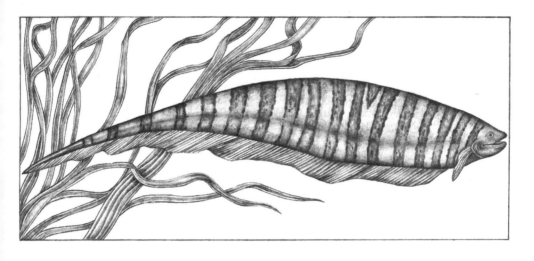

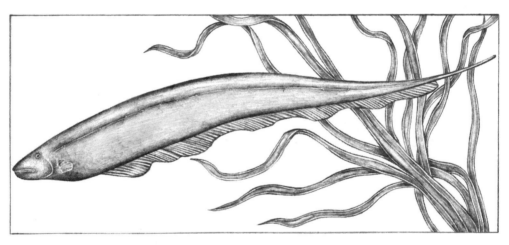

fish could use their electricity to communicate with each other. If a fish can change its electric signal, even just slightly, these changes could be used to convey information.

A scientist who was interested in learning more about how electric fish communicate with each other was Dr. Carl Hopkins. He traveled to South America in 1970 and 1971 to study some of the knife fish there. In Guyana where he worked he found thirteen different species of knife fish. Finding the fish was not difficult. Dr. Hopkins walked along the stream holding a long stick with an electrode at the end. The electrode was connected to an amplifier that Dr. Hopkins carried with him. The end of the stick with the electrode was placed in the water, and when it came near the electric fish, Dr. Hopkins heard a series of clicks.

One of the species of knife fish on which Dr. Hopkins did his experiments has the scientific name *Sternopygus macrurus*. All the Sternopygus fish have similar signals. That is, they all operate on the same "channel." However, Dr. Hopkins found that within the channel used by Sternopygus there are several subchannels. Mature male fish and mature female fish use subchannels at either end of the possible range. Immature fish use sub-

57

channels that are in between. Thus, males and females can easily identify each other's sex.

During the breeding season a male Sternopygus hides under the banks of the river where he lives. When he "hears" a female swim by, he changes his electrical signal slightly. The change tells her that he is ready to breed. If the female is ready to breed too, she will join him under the banks of the river. If two fish mate, they may learn to recognize each other's signals.

Dr. Hopkins also studied the *Eigenmannia virescens* species of knife fish in Guyana. Like Sternopygus, Eigenmannia can identify others of its own species because they are using the same channel for communication. Unlike Sternopygus, however, male and female fish do not operate on separate subchannels, although males and females may use changes in their electric signals to attract each other during the breeding season.

Eigenmannia typically fight each other when two are placed in a small aquarium. Dr. Hopkins' studies showed that they use two kinds of electric signals during their fighting. One kind of signal is made by the stronger fish. It means, "You better watch out! I'm going to fight you!" The meaning of the weaker fish's signal is, "Please don't fight me. I won't bother you."

Several other species of knife fish and numerous species of snout fish are also known to have special electric signals when they fight. Because there are so many species of weakly electric fish, scientists have not been able so far to study all of them and to find out what they are saying with their electric signals.

Why Communicate with Electricity?

Why do some fish communicate electrically? What is the advantage of an electrical system of communication? To understand the answer to these questions, one must find out where electric fish live and what they do.

The kind of place an animal lives is called its "habitat." The habitats of the knife fish, snout fish, and the Nile fish are similar, even though they live on two different continents. Both groups of fish live in shallow streams and ponds. Often the water there is muddy or murky, and it is difficult to see in it. An electric communication system is ideal in this kind of habitat. The water will transmit electric signals whether it is clear or muddy.

Thus, even when two fish cannot see each other, they can "talk" to each other with electric signals.

Weakly electric fish are typically nocturnal. During the day they hide under the banks of streams, behind rocks, or among tree roots. At night they swim out into the main part of the stream and look for food. They can communicate easily with each other at night with their electric signals. Whether it is light or dark does not matter to them.

Probably the biggest advantage of the electric communication system is that it helps fish to hide from their enemies. Because electric communication is silent and because it does not travel far (usually not more than several yards), it can be secretive. The enemies of electric fish cannot feel electric impulses. Thus, the electric fish can communicate with each other secretly and safely even in the presence of other fish. Most of the fish that are enemies of the weakly electric fish feed during the day, when the electric fish are hiding, and rest at night. Even if they did not rest at night, they would have a difficult time seeing the electric fish in the dark.

Conclusion

Every kind of living thing has special abilities that help it to adapt to its environment. Electric fish have evolved electric organs and a sensitivity to electricity. These adaptations help them to find food, to defend themselves, to locate objects, to navigate, and to communicate with each other. This ability to produce and receive electric signals is unique in the animal world.

To us the electric sense seems like a sixth sense.

We rely on our five senses—touch, taste, sight, hearing, and smell—to function in our environment. How some animals are able to use additional senses is hard for us to understand.

The study of animal behavior has revealed that there may be many more kinds of senses. Some of those that have already been discovered are the sonar of bats, the sensitivity of bees to polarized light, the sensitivity of fish to water pressure, and probably the sensitivity of birds to magnetisms. Equally amazing, the electric sense of fish provides us with another example of the various and wonderful adaptations that enable animals to survive.

INDEX *indicates illustration*

DATE DUE